small group bible studies

COURAGE TO COPE

courage to cope

10 DISCUSSIONS FOR GROUP BIBLE STUDY

MARILYN KUNZ &
CATHERINE SCHELL

MARSHALL PICKERING

William Collins Sons & Co. Ltd
London · Glasgow · Sydney · Auckland
Toronto · Johannesburg

First published in the USA in 1971 by Neighborhood
Bible Studies Inc.

This edition first published in Great Britain in 1990 by
Marshall Pickering

Marshall Pickering is an imprint of
Collins Religious Division,
part of the Collins Publishing Group
8 Grafton Street, London W1X 3LA

Printed and bound in Hong Kong

contents

contents

This topical study, *Courage to Cope*, is intended for use by adult groups that have studied a number of books of the Bible using study guides in the Small Group Bible Studies series, and for church groups in which most members are familiar with the Bible. Because this study uses selected portions of Scripture to highlight various themes, it is not recommended for people who are totally unfamiliar with the general context from which the different passages are taken.

SHARING LEADERSHIP—WHY AND HOW

Each study guide in the Small Group Bible Studies series is prepared with the intention that an adult group, by using this guide, will be able to rotate the leadership of the discussion. Those who are outgoing in personality are more likely to volunteer to lead first, but within a few weeks it should be possible for almost everyone to have the privilege of directing a discussion session.

Reasons for this approach are:

(1) The discussion leader will prepare in greater depth than the average participant.

(2) The experience of leading a study stimulates a person to be a better participant in the discussions led by others.

(3) When there is a different leader each week, group members tend to feel that the group belongs

to everyone in it; it is not "Mr. or Mrs. Smith's Bible study."

(4) The spiritually mature Christian with a wider knowledge of the Bible who is equipped to be a spiritual leader in the group is set free to *listen* to everyone in the group in a way that is not possible when leading the discussion. He (she) takes his regular turn in leading as it comes around, but if he leads the first study he must guard against the temptation to bring a great deal of outside knowledge and source material which would make others feel they could not possibly attempt to follow his example of leadership.

For study methods and discussion techniques, refer to the first booklet in this series, *How to Start a Small Group Bible Study*, as well as to the following suggestions.

HOW TO PREPARE TO PARTICIPATE IN A STUDY USING THIS GUIDE

(1) During the week before the group meeting, read carefully the Bible portions listed for the next study, keeping in mind the theme of that study. Read in at least two translations if possible.

(2) After you read the Bible passages, study through each portion using the questions in this guide book. Make brief notes of particular discoveries you wish to share with the whole group.

(3) If you take a study section each day, you can cover the discussion preparation in easy stages during the week. Use it in your daily time of meditation and prayer, asking God to teach you what he has for you in it.

(4) Use the guide questions as tools to dig deeper into the Bible passages and to help you relate your discoveries to the study theme.

(5) Review the whole study before coming to the discussion. *As an alternative* to using this study in your daily quiet time, spend at least an hour to an hour and a half in sustained study once during the week, using the above suggestions.

HOW TO PREPARE TO LEAD A STUDY

(1) Follow the above suggestions on preparing to participate in a study. Pray for wisdom and the Holy Spirit's guidance.

2) Familiarize yourself with the study guide questions until you are comfortable using them in the discussion.

(3) Try to get the movement of thought in the study, so that you are able to be flexible in using the questions.

(4) Pray for the ability to guide the discussion with love and understanding.

HOW TO LEAD A STUDY

(1) Begin with a brief prayer asking God's specific help for your study together. If you find extemporaneous prayer difficult, think through and write out your prayer ahead of time. A thoughtfully written prayer asking for God's direction can be a great help to the group. You may ask another member of the group to pray if you have asked him (her) ahead of time.

(2) Read aloud the Bible portions by the sections under which questions are grouped in the study guide. It is not necessary for everyone to read aloud, or for each to read an equal amount. Assign readers by thought units (paragraphs or larger sections).

(3) Guide the group to discover what the passages say by asking the discussion questions. Use the

suggestions from the section on "How to encourage everyone to participate."

(4) As the group studies the Bible portions together, encourage each person to be straightforward in his (her) responses. If you are sincere in your responses to Scripture, others will tend to be also.

(5) Occasionally a discussion will require two sessions. It is *not* recommended that you spend more than two sessions on one discussion. Each session should run from an hour to an hour and a half.

(6) Allow time at the end of the discussion to answer the summary questions, which help tie the whole study together.

(7) Bring the discussion to a close at the end of the time allotted. Close in prayer, using the prayer written at the end of the study if you wish.

HOW TO ENCOURAGE EVERYONE TO PARTICIPATE

(1) It is helpful to have a number of Bible translations available in the group. Encourage people to read aloud from these different translations as appropriate in the discussion.

Many translations have been used in preparation of this study guide. Particular references have been made to a few by the following abbreviations: JB—Jerusalem Bible; NEB—New English Bible; NIV—New International Version; RSV—Revised Standard Version; TEV—Today's English Version (Good News Bible); TLB—The Living Bible.

(2) Encourage discussion by asking several people to contribute answers to a question. "What do the rest of you think?" or "Is there anything else which could be added?" are ways of encouraging discussion.

(3) Be flexible and skip any questions which do not fit into the discussion as it progresses.

(4) Deal with irrelevant issues by suggesting that

the purpose of your study is to discover what is *in the Bible passage* as it relates to the topic of the discussion for the day. Suggest an informal chat about tangential or controversial issues after the regular study is dismissed.

(5) Receive all contributions warmly. Never bluntly reject what anyone says, even if you think the answer is incorrect. Instead ask in a friendly manner, "Where did you find that?" or "Is that actually what it says?" or "What do some of the rest of you think?" Allow the group to handle problems together.

(6) Be sure you don't talk too much as the leader. Redirect those questions which are asked you. A discussion should move in the form of an asterisk, back and forth between members, not in the form of a fan, with the discussion always coming back to the leader. The leader is to act as moderator. As members of a group get to know each other better, the discussion will move more freely, progressing from the fan to the asterisk pattern.

(7) Don't be afraid of pauses or silences. People need time to think about the questions and the passage. Try *never* to answer your own question— either use an alternative question or move on to another area for discussion.

(8) Watch hesitant members for an indication by facial expression or body posture that they have something to say, and then give them an encouraging nod or speak their names.

(9) Discourage too talkative members from monopolizing the discussion by specifically directing questions to others. If necessary, speak privately to the overtalkative one about the need for discussion rather than lecture in the group, and enlist his (her) aid in encouraging all to participate.

INTRODUCTION

"I can't cope!" is our cry when we're overwhelmed by circumstances beyond our control. Where do we obtain strength to handle rebellious children? Job loss? Serious illness? Leadership responsibilities in troubled times? Where *do* we find the courage to cope?

The men and women in these studies show courage as they face trying circumstances. In the midst of frustration and danger they experience the fulfillment of God's promise, *As your days, so shall your strength be* (Deuteronomy 33:25, RSV).

Acknowledging their fear and weakness, they commit themselves to the Lord who stops the mouths of lions, gives strength in persecution, comfort in sorrow, and forgiveness of sin. These men and women find that their ability to meet these situations is enhanced by persistent faith and prayer, but ultimately that the courage to cope is a gift of God.

DISCUSSION ONE
COPING WITH CHOICES

Some people spend hours deciding on which suit to buy, but give little thought to the moral and spiritual choices they make each day. Throughout the Bible we are challenged to face the meaning and consequences of our choices. We are expected to learn from the experiences of others depicted there. Whenever we are confronted with choices of spiritual importance, there *will* be a struggle.

TRUST OR DOUBT
Genesis 3:1-7

1. Ask two people to read aloud the conversation between the serpent and the woman. What means does the serpent use to tempt the woman? What line of reasoning does he pursue?
2. Between what alternatives does the woman choose?
3. What is the result of the woman's choice to doubt God and to believe the serpent? How often are our choices just as critical? Give examples of people who have made serious wrong or right choices.

LIFE OR DEATH
Deuteronomy 30:15-20

After forty years of wandering in the wilderness following their exodus from slavery in Egypt, the people of Israel are about to cross the Jordan River and enter the land God has promised them. In these verses Moses gives them final instructions.

4. What choices are set before the people of God? What will be the results of these choices?

5. What does obedience involve (verses 16a, 20)? Consider each verb carefully. What other voices are we tempted to listen to today? To what other gods are we drawn to worship?

WHO?
Mark 8:27-29

Since the beginning of his ministry, Jesus has taught his band of disciples as they traveled about together. They have listened to his teachings, watched his miracles, observed his life. This incident takes place in the closing weeks of his ministry.

6. What questions does Jesus put to his disciples? What is the difference between the questions in verses 27 and 29? How would you answer each?

7. The Gospel of Mark answers the question of who Jesus is. How do you think that men and women can be appropriately confronted with that question today?

OLD LIFE OR NEW?
Ephesians 2:1-10

8. If you had only these verses to describe the Christian faith, what would you know about it? What changes occur when a person chooses to believe in Jesus Christ and follow him?

9. From this passage, state briefly what you would tell someone who had never heard what it means to be a Christian and to live the Christian life.

10. What changes have taken place in the lives of the Colossians who believed *the true message, the Good News* (TEV) which they heard from Epaphras? Whom do they trust? Whom do they love? What hope do they have?

11. What change in life-style might be expected today in the man or woman who makes the choice to become a Christian?

12. In verses 9-12 list each of the things Paul prays for the Christians at Colossae. What choices do you think are involved for any Christian in whose life God is working in the ways outlined in these verses?

13. From this passage describe a life that is *worthy of the Lord* (NIV). What sort of life would you categorize as unworthy of the Lord?

14. How does one bear fruit (verse 10, NIV) as a Christian today? How can a person increase in the knowledge of God?

15. List all the things God does for the person who hears and believes the gospel of Christ.

Summary

1. From this study, what are the major choices to be made in life?

2. What resources are available to the Christian who wants to make wise choices in every part of life?

Prayer

Dear Lord, it was a big decision for each of us to commit our lives to you, to become Christians. Now we've discovered that that was only the beginning of the choices we must continue to make as your servants. Help us to correct and redeem the situations in which we have made wrong choices in the past and give us wisdom and strength to make right choices today. For your sake, we pray. Amen.

Today there is little or no public recognition of the existence of personal sin and guilt. Many do not recognize that sin is basically an attitude of indifference or hostility toward God, and that the acts which follow are sins against God. Paul defines the essence of sin as failure to acknowledge God as God and to worship him: "For since the creation of the world God's invisible qualities—his eternal power and divine nature—have been clearly seen ... so that men are without excuse. For although they knew God, they neither glorified him as God nor gave thanks to him" (Romans 1:20, 21, NIV).

TEMPTATION
2 Samuel 11:1-13

As a skilled general and brave warrior, David has led the Israelites in subduing their enemies, and he has united northern and southern sections of the country into one kingdom, with its capital at Jerusalem. With highways opened and trade routes restored, Israel is prosperous. At David's insistence the ark of the covenant has been brought to Jerusalem and placed in a special tabernacle, making the capital also the religious center of the land. David is a gifted poet and musician and is concerned for the services of worship to God in Israel.

The Bible gives no reason as to why David remains in Jerusalem during his army's spring campaign against the Ammonites.

1. Relate the events of this incident in your own words. At what point ought David to have turned his attention away from Bathsheba?

What similar situations today do we face as Christians? What warning signals can we learn to heed in such situations? Why do some flirt with tragedy?

2. Why would David think he had the right to take another man's wife? How do people today rationalize their behavior in similar situations?

3. What action does David take when he hears that Bathsheba is pregnant? What seems to be his intention? What contrasts do you observe between the king and his soldier Uriah? When David's first attempt fails, how does he try a second time to solve his problem?

MURDER
2 Samuel 11:14-27

4. What is David's final solution for his problem with Uriah? How do you account for such action on the part of David when for many years he refused to injure or kill King Saul who had jealously sought to destroy him?

5. What other innocent persons are destroyed because of David's sin? Give examples of how innocent bystanders suffer today because of others' sins.

6. Though David has accomplished his plan and taken Bathsheba for his wife without apparent public knowledge, who has observed his actions?

DESPISING THE WORD OF THE LORD
2 Samuel 12:1-14

7. Describe Nathan's confrontation with David. How might verses 8 and 9 read today for a Christian? What lies at the heart of sin?

8. In what ways may we be guilty of despising the laws of the Lord today? What penalty comes to David?

REPENTANCE
Psalm 51:1-19

(From its heading, note the occasion of this psalm.)

9. What requests does David make in verses 1 and 2? Upon what qualities of God's character does he dare to base his prayer?

How does your understanding of what God is like affect the way you cope with sin?

10. In verses 3-6, what does David acknowledge about himself? About God?

What difference does it make in the way you cope with sin and guilt if you recognize that there are always three parties involved: the one(s) that you have injured, yourself, and God?

11. List the verbs David uses in his request (verses 7-12). How does each request describe a different aspect of how the Lord enables us to cope with guilt?

12. What ultimate fear does sin bring (verse 11)? Contrast this with another fear that sin produces (Genesis 3:6-10).

13. Why does sin make us afraid to be with God, and afraid to be without him?

14. Notice that David does not pray for time to be rolled back to the point before he took Bathsheba, nor for Uriah to be brought to life again. What realistic approach does he take throughout this psalm? How is this essential for coping with guilt?

15. In verses 13-19, what does David ask? What does he promise? What does he understand about God?

Summary

1. Review briefly the events in David's experience of: temptation, sin, admission of guilt, repentance, forgiveness and cleansing, restoration of joyful fellowship with God.

2. What have you learned in this study about: sin's effects on the sinner, the consequences of sin (short- and long-term), the grace of God? What practical help have you gained in coping with sin and guilt in your life?

Prayer

Lord God, give us tender hearts which flee from sin as from death itself. Where we have sinned, help us to admit our sin and to face our guilt before you. Forgive us and remove our guilt, for Christ's sake. Create in us pure hearts. Put a new and loyal spirit in us. Fill us with the joy that comes from your salvation. Make our lives such that others will learn your ways and turn to you.

Biographies of most leaders reveal that at some time in their lives they have had to cope with feelings of self-doubt and inadequacy. They seemed to have been plagued with fears of the future, even after achieving success. It appears that a major difference between those who became leaders and those who did not is that the leaders moved ahead in spite of their fears.

(This study may be done in two sessions.)

MOSES—"WHO AM I?"
Exodus 3:1-12

The descendants of Jacob (Israel), enslaved for many years in Egypt, have cried to the Lord for help and he has heard their groanings. Remembering his covenant with their ancestors—Abraham, Isaac, and Jacob—God is concerned about helping them. Moses, an Israelite, was raised from infancy in the court of Pharaoh. As a young man he fled from Egypt to Midian because he killed an Egyptian whom he saw beating an Israelite. Many years now have passed, and the king of Egypt has died.

1. By what means does the Lord get Moses' attention? In what ways has God captured your attention for a job he wants you to undertake?

2. How does God identify himself to Moses? What effect does this have on Moses?

23

3. Note all the verbs in verses 7-10 that describe the activity of the Lord. How does Moses respond to God's command to go to Pharaoh and bring the Israelites out of Egypt? With whose power is Moses more impressed? Why, do you think?

4. How should God's answer (verse 12) be sufficient for Moses or for anyone whom the Lord calls to serve him?

Why do we, like Moses, automatically do a resource inventory which leaves God out? If we, like Moses, still have fears when God says, "But I will be with you," is that humility or arrogance on our part?

MOSES—"GET SOMEONE ELSE"
Exodus 4:10-17

5. In answer to Moses' objection in 4:1, "What if the Egyptians don't believe me or listen to me?," the Lord gives him three miraculous signs that he may use as proof to validate his message.

What new difficulty does Moses foresee if he obeys God's call (verse 10)?

6. What is the Lord's answer to this objection? Why, do you think, doesn't God simply get someone else instead of Moses?

What kinds of responses do you make to a challenge to take a leadership role? How do you avoid taking such responsibility?

7. How does the Lord react to Moses' plea to send someone else? Sometimes the Lord may accede to our request and give us an Aaron, but it is not his first and best choice for us. If God gives us leadership opportunities, how can we trust him for the ability needed to fulfill them?

JOSHUA—REPLACING A STRONG LEADER
Joshua 1:1-15

Imagine your feelings if you were chosen to take the place of the chief executive of your company or the head of your university, the top-ranking general of the army, or the leader of your country. These are probably some of the feelings Joshua has as he faces the task of leading the Israelites into the promised land.

8. List all the promises and all the commands God gives to Joshua in verses 1-9. In what sort of situation does one keep saying, "Be strong and of good courage"? Note the promise in verse 3.

9. How is Joshua to use this *Book of the law* (verse 8)?

10. What do you learn about Joshua from his words and actions in verses 10-15? What has he learned about obedience and trust in God from Moses, whom he served as aide during the forty years in the wilderness?

(If you wish to handle this discussion in two sessions, plan to divide the study at this point. At the beginning of the second session, review briefly what you discovered in the first session.)

GIDEON—TAKING A STAND AGAINST EVIL
Judges 6:1-39

For about 170 years following the death of Joshua, the tribes of Israel were united only by their common faith in God. Whenever they turned to follow other gods, they became weak and divided, easy prey to the peoples around them. Gideon is one of a series of twelve leaders *(judges)* during this time, raised up by the Lord to deliver his people from their enemies.

11. Describe the situation in Israel (verses 1-6).

12. In verses 7-10, how does the Lord respond to the Israelites' cry for help? What actions on their part have led to their oppression by the Midianites?

13. How do you think that the emotional and spiritual climate of a nation affects an individual living in it?

14. Read verses 11-24 as a drama. Ask two individuals to read the parts of the angel of the Lord and of Gideon, and a narrator to read verses 11, 19, 21, 24.

15. What questions does Gideon raise in his conversation with the angel of the Lord (the Lord himself)? What doubts does he express?

If you are asked to undertake a specific task, what kinds of questions do you raise? Why?

16. Read verses 25-40, assigning people to the parts of the townspeople and Joash. Have the narrator read the connecting verses.

17. Compare the task Gideon thinks he is about to undertake (verse 14) with his first assignment (verses 25, 26).

How do you react if it turns out that more is involved in a project than you first thought? What suggests the danger of the situation?

How does the religious situation in Gideon's town show the accuracy of the Lord's words through his prophet in verse 10?

18. How would Gideon's actions against Baal worship be a necessary preparation for leading the tribes of Israel against the gathering forces of their enemies?

19. How is Gideon empowered for his task (verse

34)? As he makes preparations for battle, of what does he want to be absolutely certain?

When do you react in a way similar to Gideon? How do you discern whether you are being humble or you are acting in unbelief?

20. What simple test does Gideon propose? How does God answer?

21. Describe Gideon: his background, his evaluation of himself and his abilities, his growing relationship with the Lord, his attitudes and actions, his development as a leader.

TIMOTHY
2 Timothy 1:6-14

Timothy is a young man of mixed Jewish and Greek background, converted to Christ during Paul's first missionary journey. He later traveled with Paul. He has been left by Paul as a pastor of the church in Ephesus to warn those teaching false doctrines and to call them back to sincere Christian living. Imprisoned in Rome, Paul writes to *my son whom I love, who is faithful in the Lord* (1 Corinthians 4:17).

22. Under what circumstances are you likely to be afraid? Fainthearted? Nervous? Apprehensive? Vacillating and weak? Discouraged? Give specific examples.

23. From this passage, list all that God has done for us. What has he entrusted to us? With Timothy, what are we as Christians called to do?

24. If God gives us a spirit of power, of love, and of self-discipline (self-control), how can we exercise this spirit in our leadership responsibilities? What sort of leader would this combination of qualities produce?

Summary

What feelings and attitudes do Moses, Joshua, Gideon, and Timothy seem to have in common? How is each able to cope with his fears and to function as a leader?

Prayer

In the Old Testament, Isaiah seems to be the only one who said, "Here am I, send me." So many others, like me, seem to be saying, "Not me, Lord, get someone else." So Lord, you don't have a group of volunteers, but you have drafted us for service. Often we come kicking and screaming into the front lines. Help us, Lord, to cope with the responsibility of leadership. Be with us.

Forgive us when we are tempted to cowardice. Anoint us with your spirit of love and power and self-control. Thank you that the power of your Spirit is available to us. Strengthen our resolve to serve you faithfully.

DISCUSSION FOUR
COPING WITH PERSECUTION

To persecute means to pursue, to injure, to cause to suffer because of religious belief. The history of the Christian church from Stephen (Acts 7) until now, records the experiences of countless men and women willing to lay their lives on the line for the name of Jesus Christ. These heroes of the church include many who left their homes to travel to distant lands and other cultures with the gospel, and who suffered rejection and even death.

PERSECUTION UNDER THE SOVEREIGNTY OF GOD
Matthew 5:10-12; Romans 12:14

1. What kinds of difficulty does Jesus predict for his followers? For what reason will they be persecuted?

2. What rewards belong to those who suffer for Christ's sake? To what honored company does the persecuted Christian belong?

3. In Romans 12:14 what "normal" reaction to persecution does Paul reject? What unique opportunity does the Christian have?

4. What injury, insult, or suffering have you experienced because of your faith in Christ?

A TIME TO BEAR TESTIMONY
Luke 21:10-19

5. For what kinds of experiences does Jesus prepare his followers? What unusual opportunities will persecution bring?

6. What types of persecution do Christians face today in your town? In other parts of the world?

7. Why do you think Jesus tells his followers not to prepare their defense beforehand? What response should you give to someone who is anti-Christian and who challenges your faith? What does Jesus promise (verses 15, 18, 19)?

8. As you consider the possibility of facing criticism or worse because you are a Christian, what difference does it make to you that God is ruler over all?

PAUL'S TRIAL
Acts 24:1, 5-21

9. What accusations are made against Paul? What does he deny? What does he admit?

10. Notice the ways in which Paul's experience illustrates Jesus' predictions in Luke 21. What fulfillment do you see of Jesus' promise in Luke 21:15?

THE LOVE OF GOD
Romans 8:35-39

11. What questions does Paul put to his readers? Why may troubles, including persecution, make us feel cut off from the Lord's help?

12. According to verses 37-39, what confidence can the Christian have during times of persecution?

TESTS OF FAITH
1 Peter 1:3-9

13. What reasons for rejoicing does every Christian have (verses 3-5)? Compare the duration of *trials* (verse 6) and the duration of the Christian's *inheritance* (verse 4).

14. What purpose do trials accomplish (verses 6, 7)?

What does comparing persecution for one's faith to the refining of gold reveal about the severity and the duration of the trial? The benefits of the outcome? How would knowing this help you to cope with persecution?

15. Why does persecution validate faith? What experiences have you had which made you aware of the genuineness of your faith in Christ?

16. In the midst of the sadness and grief that trials bring, what other emotions does the Christian experience (verses 8, 9)? Why?

EXPECT PERSECUTION
1 Peter 4:12-19

17. Read this section in the NIV and TEV. If we view painful trials for our faith as sharing in Christ's sufferings, what responses to trials are appropriate (verses 12, 13)?

18. If one is insulted because he or she follows Christ, what does this indicate (verse 14)?

19. What should a Christian not be guilty of (verse 15)?

20. In what ways do you make it known that you are a Christian? If you suffer for *bearing the name of Christ* (verse 16, JB), what reaction should you have?

21. What point does Peter make by the questions he raises in verses 17 and 18?

22. In view of all that has been said in verses 12-18, what two things ought a Christian do who is suffering because it is God's will (verse 19)?

What practices do you think help us to develop coping skills so that if we should face persecution for being a Christian, we can do so with courage?

Summary

1. Outline the defense that you would use if you were faced with a situation comparable to what Paul faced in Acts 24. To what would you plead guilty? Of what would you declare yourself innocent?

2. What are God's promises to you if you suffer because you are a Christian?

3. What are the rewards of suffering for your faith in Christ?

Prayer

Lord Jesus, we confess that many of us fear the ridicule of a sneer or a raised eyebrow more than Paul feared the power of the Roman Empire. We do not experience persecution because we do not publicly confess our faith and stand for righteousness. Deliver us from cowardice, Lord. The cause of Christ in our generation is in need of heroes. Grant us wisdom. Grant us courage. Make our lives a bold and loving witness to your name.

DISCUSSION FIVE
COPING WITH FAMILY PROBLEMS

Many parents whose children rebel against the moral standards and faith of their family experience grief so deep that they cannot talk about it. The church must develop appropriate settings in which adults facing complex family problems can see how the Bible speaks to their needs, and can help one another to work out problems. Instead of dissipating their energies in blame and recrimination, men and women need help to confront their problems directly.

JOYS AND DISAPPOINTMENTS
1 Samuel 1:1-18

Samuel lived at the end of the time of the judges in Israel. His period of office may be dated from about 1075 to 1035 B.C. It was he who anointed Saul and then David to be king over Israel.

1. Describe the family of Elkanah. What is a continuing cause of friction within this family? What are the underlying causes of conflicts in families today?

Note—Under the law of Moses, a man could have more than one wife, but it was not God's original intention, and the situation could cause great misery.

2. How does Elkanah try to comfort and help Hannah? What sort of person does Peninnah seem to be? What practical ways can you suggest to work within a situation whose basic framework cannot be changed? See Galatians 5:26; Ephesians 4:32.

3. Compare Hannah's prayer with Numbers 6:1-5. What promise does she make to the Lord? How does Eli misinterpret Hannah's actions? What is her explanation?

4. How is Hannah encouraged by her visit to worship the Lord at Shiloh? When you truly commit your problem to the Lord, what difference does it make in your attitude?

A PRAYER ANSWERED
1 Samuel 1:19-28

5. When does the Lord begin to answer Hannah's prayer? What is the meaning of the name *Samuel?*

Note—Samuel became the last of the judges of Israel and the first of the Old Testament prophets. See 1 Samuel 3:19-21.

6. Since infants were weaned much later then than they are today, Hannah would have had several years to teach Samuel. What spiritual training do you think Hannah gives her son? What do you imagine it costs her to keep her vow? How do you think she is able to cope with leaving Samuel in Eli's care?

SACRILEGE
1 Samuel 2:11-26

7. Contrast the way in which Samuel develops under Eli's tutelage and the way Eli's sons have turned out. What are the sons of Eli doing? What would be a comparable situation today?

8. How does Eli try to control his sons' wickedness? For God's evaluation of how Eli handled his sons, see 1 Samuel 3:13, 14.

What tragedies occur today in the lives of young adults who will not listen? When should one start to teach children to listen to their parents' teaching?

9. How would you differentiate between the normal learning to stand on one's own feet which every child experiences, and a pattern of rebellion which becomes destructive to the child and to others?

ABSALOM'S CONSPIRACY
2 Samuel 15:1-18; 16:15, 20-22

Soon after David's sin in the matter of Bathsheba and Uriah, the prophet Nathan's predictions of evil in David's house have begun to come true. David's eldest son Amnon rapes his half-sister Tamar, and her brother Absalom avenges her ill-treatment by arranging Amnon's murder. After a period of banishment, Absalom has been received again by his father the king.

10. What clever plan of action does Absalom develop (15:1-6)? Of what weakness in David's kingdom does he take advantage? With what result?

11. What are the next steps in Absalom's conspiracy? What lie does he tell his father? Why is this a particularly cruel lie? How does he also deceive his guests?

12. What humiliation does David experience in 15:13-18 and in 16:15, 20-22? Compare this to Nathan's prophecy in 12:10-12. Why is being humiliated and betrayed by a family member so difficult to handle?

GRIEF
2 Samuel 18:31—19:8

13. When David's attempt to protect Absalom's life fails, what is his reaction? What problem does this cause David's loyal servants?

How do other children in a family react today when a rebellious child gets all the attention?

14. Why and how does Joab remonstrate with the king? How does David respond? What do you think it costs David to "pull himself together" for the sake of those who love him?

Summary

1. Review how Elkanah, Hannah, Eli, and David cope with their family problems.

2. What have you learned from their successes and failures about how and how not to handle family conflict? The discipline of children? Conflict between parent and adult child?

Prayer

Lord, we ask for wisdom and strength, patience and faith in raising our children to honor and obey you. We pray that our children will hear your voice and respond as young Samuel did, "Speak, Lord, for your servant is listening." May we be examples to our children of men and women who obey you in every aspect of life.

DISCUSSION SIX
COPING WITH PRESSURE, CONFLICT,
AND EXHAUSTION

A modern expression is "burnout," but the experience is not new. Men and women throughout history have had to deal with all sorts of pressures and conflicts, and their frequent result—exhaustion.

Expressions such as "the straw that broke the camel's back" picture the accumulation of burdens until the smallest addition is too much. Learning to cope with pressure is essential for survival. Awareness that God knows and cares is one of the first steps in handling the problem.

(This discussion may be done in two sessions.)

AHAB
1 Kings 16:29-33; 17:1

Ahab, of the dynasty of Omri, reigned over the northern kingdom of Israel from about 874 to 853 B.C.

1. What changes for the worse take place in Israel as a result of Ahab's ascent to power? How does the Lord, the God of Israel, view Ahab's actions?

2. What claim and what prediction does Elijah make? Contrast who is served in 16:31 and 17:1. Why is conflict between Ahab and Elijah inevitable?

DROUGHT
1 Kings 17:2-24

3. Describe the pressures Elijah faces during the prolonged drought that follows his declaration in verse 1. What provisions does the Lord make for his servant? For the widow and her child?

Ask members of your study group to briefly share instances of deprivation that they or people they know have experienced.

4. What does the healing of her child reveal to the widow? What encouragement would this incident be to Elijah?

TROUBLER OF ISRAEL
1 Kings 18:1-21

5. Describe Obadiah. What planning and courage must it have taken for a man in his position to hide a hundred prophets of the Lord when the queen was on a campaign to destroy them all? What does Obadiah fear if he reports Elijah's presence to King Ahab?

What kinds of pressures, overt and subtle, are felt by a person who lives for God under a government which encourages the destruction of the Christian faith?

6. Using verses 17-19, contrast the trouble that Elijah brought to Israel with that brought on Israel by Ahab. What does Elijah command Ahab to do? Why do you think that Ahab obeys?

7. What is Elijah's challenge to the people of Israel as they assemble at Mount Carmel? What does the silence of the people indicate to Elijah?

THE CONTEST
1 Kings 18:22-40

8. Imagine yourself in a situation in which you stand alone for your faith. What stress do you experience? Why?

9. Describe what happens on Mount Carmel. Consider the physical and emotional energy Elijah expends during this day. What do you think are the emotions that Elijah experiences?

10. In contrast to the frenzied dancing and shouting of Baal's prophets, how and what does Elijah pray? What is the outcome of the contest between Baal and the Lord of Israel? Compare verses 21 and 39, 40.

11. Think of an experience demanding great physical and emotional strength. How did you feel once the pressure was off?

THE RACE
1 Kings 18:41-46

12. Read 17:1 and 18:1 with this section. What is involved for Elijah in finishing the situation begun in 17:1? What bold message does he give to Ahab?

13. Running before Ahab to Jezreel was the act of a loyal servant, public testimony that Elijah was not opposing the king as ruler of the land but rather was seeking to win him to worship the Lord.

By what power does Elijah run the seventeen miles to Jezreel?

(If you wish to handle this discussion in two sessions, plan to divide the study here. Begin the second session with a brief review of the events in Elijah's life up to this point.)

REST AND RECUPERATION
1 Kings 19:1-21

14. It has been decisively demonstrated on Mount Carmel that the Lord, not Baal, is the only God. The 450 prophets of Baal have been put to death, and a torrential rain has broken the long drought. What sort of response to these events do you think Elijah may have expected from Ahab and Jezebel?

15. What does Jezebel do when she hears from Ahab all that has happened? Why do you think she is able to frighten Elijah?

16. Contrast Elijah's experience in 18:40-46 with that in 19:1-4. How severe is his depression?

17. If you were Elijah's counselor, how would you respond to what he tells you in 19:3, 4, 10, 14?

18. What provisions does the Lord make for his exhausted and depressed servant? What part do adequate rest and nourishing food play in healing someone like Elijah? How is God preparing Elijah to face his situation?

19. Horeb (Mount Sinai) was the place where God spoke to Moses and gave his covenant to the people of Israel. The cave in verse 9 may be the cleft in the rock of Exodus 33:22.

How do you account for the question the Lord asks Elijah in verses 9 and 13? What is Elijah's answer in both instances? What seems to be his mental and emotional state at this point?

20. Though God revealed his presence to Moses in the earthquake, storm, and lightning (Exodus 19:16-20), these are only indicators of his coming before he speaks to Elijah in a gentle whisper. Considering Elijah's mental and emotional state, how is this appropriate?

21. How does the Lord deal with Elijah's feelings of futility and aloneness? In what way is the reality of

the situation (verse 18) different from Elijah's perception of it? Have you ever had an incorrect perception of a major problem you were facing? Why was your perception inaccurate?

22. How does the Lord reveal to Elijah that the future does not depend solely on the prophet's ability to bring about change?

23. Why are we sometimes ambivalent about getting the help we need? How does Elijah indicate that he is willing to have a helper?

Summary

1. Which of Elijah's pressures were real and which were imagined? How can you learn to discern the difference in your own situation?

2. List each of the helpers the Lord provided for Elijah. Make a list of the helpers that the Lord has provided for you in times of need.

Prayer

Lord God, we don't have to deal with Ahab or Jezebel, but sometimes we have to cope with people who can make life miserable for us and for others. We may not have a three-year drought in the land, but we do experience personal droughts and we worry about economic survival. We are under pressures, real and imagined. Help us to seek and to accept the provisions you have for us. Thank you for the promise the Lord Jesus made to his disciples, "Come to me, all you who are weary and burdened, and I will give you rest."

Does anyone ever give you a hard time because you are a Christian? In many parts of the world today, men and women who actively attempt to communicate the message of Christ encounter not only criticism but hardship and danger. The experiences of Paul and his companions, the methods they used, and the message they proclaimed deserve careful study by every concerned Christian in our day.

CORINTH
Acts 18:1-11

On his second missionary journey, Paul endures beating and imprisonment in Philippi. His ministry in Thessalonica and Berea is disturbed by mobs stirred up by unbelieving Jews who followed him from one city to the other. After preaching to Jews and Gentiles in the synagogue and marketplace in Athens, Paul comes to Corinth about A.D. 50. This city in Achaia (southern Greece), a trading center in the Roman world, is noted for its temple to Aphrodite, the goddess of love, and the sexual immorality connected with it.

1. From verses 1-5, list four or five things that you observe about the life of the early Christians who sought to serve the Lord in the midst of the Roman Empire.

2. What difficulties and what encouragement does Paul have in Corinth? Considering what happened previously in Thessalonica and Berea when men and

women in the synagogues believed his message, what may Paul expect will soon happen to him and his team in Corinth? How might such expectation influence their plans and their morale?

3. If you were in Paul's situation, how would the Lord's message in a vision affect your attitude and future activities in Corinth?

A MISSIONARY LETTER
2 Corinthians 4

This letter from Paul to the young Corinthian church was probably written from Macedonia (northern Greece) about six years after he first visited Corinth.

4. Ask one person (representing the Apostle Paul) to read this chapter aloud from a contemporary translation while the other members of the group make notes on the words and ideas which are repeated or contrasted. Share your observations.

What is the mood of this chapter?

DEFENSE
2 Corinthians 4:1-12

5. What accusations does Paul seem to be answering in verses 2-5?

6. According to verse 1, why are Paul and Timothy able to continue to serve Christ? When are you as a Christian tempted to become discouraged and to lose heart?

7. What does it mean to *distort* or *tamper with the word of God* (NIV, RSV)? Why would someone proclaiming the Christian message be tempted to do this?

What can you do when you observe that someone

is trying to make the Bible say more, or less, than it does in a particular section?

8. Recognizing what Paul says here, how would you handle a situation in which people excuse using deceitful methods to communicate the gospel, saying that "the end justifies the means"?

9. What keeps people from believing the gospel of Christ? By whom and how will the truth be revealed to them?

Recognizing this, what must we preach and what must we not preach? How can you distinguish as to which you (or others) are preaching?

10. From the word picture Paul uses in verse 7, what do you learn about the gospel message and about those who carry it?

11. By what series of contrasts does Paul describe the difficult experiences he and Timothy have faced in their ministry? Sum up how Paul views all his experiences. In each situation, whose death and whose life is being revealed?

12. Share a present-day situation in which you have seen the life of Jesus revealed in the life of someone you know.

AN ETERNAL GLORY
2 Corinthians 4:13-18

13. Read verse 1 with this section. What motivates Paul and Timothy to persevere in their ministry? What are you doing so that more and more people may receive the grace of God in Jesus Christ?

14. What reasons does Paul give for not losing heart in spite of all the difficulties experienced in proclaiming the gospel?

15. List the four contrasts which conclude this chapter. What perspective does this give you on your

current problems? What means of daily inner renewal are open to every Christian? (See Psalm 1:2, 3; Philippians 4:4-7.)

Summary

1. What goals and attitudes does Paul state for his ministry? If your church, denomination, or mission organization would use the Scriptures in this study for recommended attitudes and practices, what changes might there be?

2. How might some contemporary methods of communicating the gospel be changed if underhanded ways were abolished?

Prayer

Lord, help us not to become discouraged in your service. May we give ourselves as fully to communicating the gospel to our generation as Paul did to his. Go before us to the needy places, to the Corinths of today, to those without the light of Christ. We praise you for the power of the gospel to dispel darkness, to bring light to those blinded by the god of this age. Thank you that the frailty of our bodies and the difficulties in our lives can be the means you use to bring the resurrection life of Jesus to many people.

DISCUSSION EIGHT
COPING WITH OPPRESSION

Oppression is defined as the unjust or cruel exercise of authority or power by imposing burdens. Tyrannical oppression may crush the spirit, the mind, or the body. Living in a repressive or an immoral society puts many people under oppression, but the psalmist encourages his hearers: "The Lord is a refuge for the oppressed, a stronghold in times of trouble" (Psalm 9:9, NIV).

JESUS THE DELIVERER
Luke 4:13-21

1. In saying that the passage from Isaiah is now fulfilled, what claims does Jesus make? For whom is the Lord especially concerned?

2. What will Jesus do for each group mentioned? Who are the captives or prisoners in our society?

From what oppression do you need release? What things hold captive people whom you know?

THE LORD ALMIGHTY SAYS
Zechariah 7:9, 10; 8:16, 17; Malachi 3:5

3. What message from the Lord do these prophets proclaim? What does the Lord forbid? What does he desire?

4. What groups of people are especially vulnerable in a society where justice, righteousness, and compassion do not operate?

5. Bring news articles to illustrate the sins in our day against which Zechariah and Malachi both warn.

SPIRITUAL OPPRESSION
Mark 2:27—3:6

In Jesus' time the Sabbath was hedged with over a thousand man-made rules, making a terrible burden of the day which had been given for people's physical and spiritual benefit.

6. How do the Pharisees view the matter of keeping the Sabbath? But what does Jesus make the issue?

7. What is the Pharisees' attitude toward the man with the withered hand? In contrast, how does Jesus treat him? What does it cost Jesus to do this?

8. What is Jesus' reaction to the hard and stubborn hearts of these religious leaders?

9. By his attitude and actions here, how does Jesus treat the oppressed and the oppressors?

SPIRITUAL OPPRESSION AND FREEDOM
Galatians 5:1-10, 13-15

Christ has fulfilled the law in his death on the cross. Those who trust in Christ have been set free from trying to earn right standing before God by the impossible task of perfectly obeying the whole law. Someone apparently was telling the Galatian Christians that they needed to be circumcised, but this would have put them under the bondage from which Christ had delivered them.

10. In what two ways may spiritual freedom be lost (verses 2-4, 13, 15)?

11. Some religious teachers and leaders enslave their followers today. For what warning signs mentioned in this passage ought Christians to keep alert?

12. What will happen if Christians use their freedom

to please themselves? How may one person's "freedom" oppress another person?

How is Christian freedom to be expressed (verses 6, 13)? What basic guideline for relating to others does Paul emphasize (verse 14)?

PHYSICAL OPPRESSION
Matthew 5:38-41

13. What three illustrations of oppression does Jesus give (verses 39-41)? In the first two instances, what is likely to happen if one retaliates in kind?

14. What attitude would be the usual response of a person in the situation in verse 41?

Note—Under Roman rule, any Jew in Palestine could be compelled by the command of a Roman soldier to carry a burden for one mile.

15. Instead of "tit for tat," what sort of attitude does Jesus expect his followers to exercise in response to personal insult (verse 39)? Infringement of one's rights (verse 40)? Compelled service (verse 41)?

16. If one obeys Jesus' commands here, what power does this give the victim over his or her oppressor?

17. What reasons does Jesus give for loving your enemy and praying for those who persecute you?

Summary

1. Describe acts of oppression (large or small) which you have experienced, seen, or heard about this week. Why were the oppressors able to oppress?

2. From this study, what have you learned about God's attitude toward oppression? Toward the oppressed? Toward the oppressor?

3. What responsibility and what opportunities do you have as a Christian to change oppressive social

and spiritual conditions in your community? In this nation? In other countries?

Prayer

Thank you, Lord Jesus, that you have come to deliver all who are oppressed. Give us a concern for the oppressed in our world. Grant us courage and wisdom to take action on their behalf.

Deliver us from anyone who would try to play god in our lives and enslave us spiritually. Help us to recognize and resist the oppressor in whatever guise he or she comes.

Remove from our hearts, Lord, every inclination to oppress others. Thank you that in your service we are free to grow and mature in character until we are like our Father in heaven.

DISCUSSION NINE
COPING WITH WORK PRESSURES
AND DISAPPOINTMENTS

Six days you shall labor and do all your work
(Exodus 20:9, NIV). Though work can be a source of
great joy and satisfaction, pressures and disappointments are also part of every job. It is often what
one does in the face of these that determines success
or failure.

Modern society tends to overemphasize the money
paid for work rather than the quality of work done,
or what that work accomplishes. It is time for
Christian men and women to rethink our concept of
work, to make spiritual values the basis of job
success. As you study the incidents in this discussion
in the life of Daniel and of Jeremiah, evaluate your
own attitudes and actions.

(This study may be done in two sessions.)

Daniel 6
(Read the entire chapter before discussing it by sections.)

The king of Babylon besieged Jerusalem in 605
B.C. Along with other members of the nobility and
royal court of Judah, a young man named Daniel was
taken hostage to Babylon where he and other young
Israelites were trained for the king's service. Eventually
the king made Daniel *ruler over the entire province
of Babylon and placed him in charge of all its
wise men* (2:48, NIV). Darius the Mede conquered

Babylon in 539 B.C. when Daniel must have been about eighty years old.

OPPORTUNITY FOR JOB ADVANCEMENT
Daniel 6:1-9

1. Describe the administrative structure of Darius' kingdom, and its purpose. How does Daniel fare? Why is the king considering Daniel for the top position?

Note—A *satrap* (NIV) is a Persian or Median noble who rules over a province.

2. In what terms do you think that *an excellent spirit* and *exceptional qualities* (verse 3, RSV, NIV) would be described in government or in business today? What virtues do you think would be sought in the time of Darius and today? What does Darius plan for Daniel?

3. In verses 4 and 5, what seems to motivate the *presidents* (administrators) and *satraps* (KJV, NIV)? Why will it not be easy to remove Daniel from the competition for the position of ruler over the whole kingdom?

What one hope do these men have? What sort of person might be equally difficult to undermine in your place of work?

4. What do you think motivates Darius to sign the decree? What happens in a society if those in charge are not aware of the ramifications of their decisions?

LOYALTY TEST
Daniel 6:10-28

5. Imagine yourself in a position comparable to Daniel's, with the highest position in the land almost within your reach. What temptation would there be

to rationalize that conforming to this temporary decree is for "the greater glory of God"?

6. What does Daniel do when he hears of the decree (verses 10, 11)? What is he risking? How difficult would it be for you to give thanks in that situation?

7. What is the foundation of Daniel's life, the basis of his value system? Give an example of someone struggling with value judgments on his or her job today.

8. How do Daniel's enemies protect their interests? By what is the king ruled? In what way is the moral uprightness of Daniel and the king an advantage to Daniel's enemies? What evidence is there that your "enemies" and friends can rely on your moral and spiritual integrity?

9. What does the king's prayer reveal about the life that Daniel has lived before the king? How does the king pray (verse 16)?

10. How is the Lord honored by Daniel's experience in the den of lions (verses 18, 22)? By Darius' decree (verses 25-28)?

Note—*A lions' den* (verse 16) was a pit where large numbers of lions were kept, from which they would be released for the royal lion hunts.

(If you wish to handle this study in two sessions, plan to divide it at this point. At the beginning of the second session, review briefly what you learned in the first session.)

Jeremiah 36
(Read the entire chapter before discussing it by sections.)

Josiah, responsible for great religious reform and renewal, was the best king that Judah ever had. He *turned to the Lord with all his heart and with all his soul and with all his strength* (2 Kings 23:25, NIV). Jeremiah began his ministry as the prophet of the Lord in 627 B.C. in the thirteenth year of King Josiah's reign. After Josiah was killed in a battle with Egypt in 609 B.C., Jeremiah faced constant opposition from the political and religious leaders of Judah.

GATHERING THE DATA
Jeremiah 36:1-8

11. What is the purpose of the Lord's message to Jeremiah? What is to be recorded on the scroll? Why can't the prophet deliver the message to the people?

12. How and when does Jeremiah arrange for the people to hear the Lord's message? What frustration do you think Jeremiah feels in not being able to deliver the message himself?

13. What have you learned when you have had to entrust an important responsibility to another person?

THE PRESENTATION
Jeremiah 36:9-19

14. Describe the setting (verses 6-8) for the reading of the scroll. How do you imagine Baruch feels as he reads the message from the Lord to all the people?

15. What action does Micaiah take upon hearing the contents of the scroll? How do the princes (officials) respond? What does their advice to Baruch and Jeremiah (verse 19) indicate about conditions in the kingdom?

16. In what ways have you seen attempts at reform resisted in the place where you work, or in the church? What actions have you taken to cope with such situations? What were the results?

REVIEW AND REJECTION
Jeremiah 36:20-26

17. How does the king respond to the criticism in the scroll? How do you account for such different reactions on the part of the king and his attendants to the reading of the scroll? What appropriate reactions do not occur?

18. What attempt is made to save the scroll? How do you think that we are judged by the Lord when we fail to listen, be afraid, and rend our garments in the face of conditions today? What evil goes uncorrected today?

PROPOSAL RESUBMITTED AND EXPANDED
Jeremiah 36:27-32

19. Put yourself in the place of Jeremiah and Baruch. How do you feel when you learn of the king's reaction to the Lord's message, and that the scroll has been destroyed? What enables you to begin again?

How do you cope with disappointments and disasters in your work?

20. Why is the second scroll longer? What new words of judgment are added?

Summary

1. How do you think that the people of their day judged Daniel? Jeremiah?

2. What perspective does this study give you on the difficult situations and decisions you face in your own life?

Prayer

Lord, we have to do things we don't like to do.
Every job has some negative aspects, some lions to
face. Grant that we may have the courage of Daniel
and the tenacity of Jeremiah and Baruch. Keep us
from taking the easy way out when confrontation is
called for. Deliver us from sacrificing truth and
righteousness to gain success in any job.

Everyone experiences loneliness. The young and the old feel it intensely. The saddest aspect of aging is not loss of physical strength, but loss of meaningful relationships. Coping with loneliness, with aging, and with death, is seldom discussed, but the struggle goes on just below the surface in many lives.

LONELINESS
Psalm 27:7-10, 14

1. What requests does the psalmist make of the Lord? What do these verses reveal about him? About his understanding of God?

2. In what ways do people sometimes "hide their faces" from one another? What loneliness does the psalmist imagine in verse 10? What does it mean to be forsaken?

3. From this psalm, what action would you recommend to someone who feels deserted and abandoned? What does the psalmist advise in verse 14?

AGING PATRIARCH
Joshua 14:6-14

Of the twelve men sent into Canaan to explore the land in preparation for the entry of the Israelites, only Caleb and Joshua urged that they immediately take possession of the land because the Lord was with them. The people's failure to trust God meant forty years were spent in the wilderness until the adult generation responsible for that decision had died.

4. What is the testimony of the eighty-five-year-old Caleb? What has motivated him throughout his life? Why is he prepared at this age to take on a new challenge? Why do you think that he is still unafraid of the Anakim (Anakites)?

5. How do you think that someone's personal faith and outlook on life affects the aging process?

AGING KING
1 Chronicles 29:10-19

After ruling Israel for forty years, David hands over the kingdom to his young son Solomon before the assembly of his people. He acknowledges Solomon as the one God has chosen to build the temple at Jerusalem.

6. What understanding of God does King David reveal in verses 10-13?

7. What does David acknowledge about himself, his people, and their possessions? Why can't he take credit for preparing what is needed to build the temple?

8. With what attitude does David bring all the treasure for the temple before the Lord? What is his prayer for his people and for Solomon? Compare with Caleb's attitude. What does it mean to live a lifetime wholly following the Lord?

DEATH
John 11:21-27

9. Lazarus, brother of Mary and Martha, has been buried for four days when Jesus arrives in Bethany. How is Martha handling the death of her brother?

What does she believe Jesus could have done? How does she respond to Jesus' statement that her brother will rise again?

10. In answer to Martha, what stupendous claim does Jesus make? How does he validate his claim in verses 38-44? How does Jesus' power over death affect the way you feel about death?

ANGUISH OF DEATH
Mark 14:32-42

11. As a ballet master how would you choreograph these events in Gethsemane to express the feelings of Jesus and his disciples? Describe body movements which would express their emotion.

12. How does the Gospel writer emphasize Jesus' aloneness? What is his prayer? How is it answered?

13. Why don't the disciples stay awake with Jesus? Why do you think that they don't know how to answer him? When have you found yourself like the disciples in a similar situation with a friend?

PAUL FACES DEATH
2 Timothy 4:6-18

14. How does Paul view his coming death (verses 6-8)? What gives him satisfaction? What does he expect at the Lord's coming?

15. What do verses 9-18 reveal about Paul's situation? What are his concerns? Why is Paul alone except for Luke? In view of this, why isn't he distraught? Of what is Paul confident?

VICTORY OVER DEATH
Hebrews 2:9, 14, 15; 1 Corinthians 15:20-26

16. According to the letter to the Hebrews, what did Jesus accomplish for us by his death? What does

it mean that Jesus delivers from the fear of death? What aspects of death has he overcome on our behalf?

17. How does Paul describe Christ's victory over death in his letter to Corinth? What will prevent death from having the final word? What practical help does Christ's resurrection give you in handling the fear of death?

Summary

1. Since few people escape the experiences of loneliness and of aging, and no one escapes death, how can we prepare to cope with these experiences?

2. From this study, what answers would Caleb, David, and Paul give to this question?

Prayer

Lord, as you were with David, Caleb, Martha, Paul, so be with us. Meet us at the moments when we pray that someone will come to us to ease our loneliness. Strengthen us to reach out to others who may be lonely. Help us to bear the aches and pains of aging bodies with grace and courage. Fill our mouths with your praise to declare your splendor. Help us to declare your power to the next generation. Be near us in the hour of our dying, and grant us the sure and certain hope of resurrection.

NOTES

Marshall Pickering is engaged in a programme of making Marilyn Kunz's and Catherine Schell's group Bible Study outlines, which were originally published in the USA, more widely available in the UK. New titles will be added regularly to the list of titles currently available. The authors suggest the following study guide:

RECOMMENDED FOR SMALL GROUP DISCUSSION BIBLE STUDY

New Groups and Outreach Groups

Mark (recommended as first unit of study)
Acts
John, Book 1 (Chaters 1–10)
John, Book 2 (Chapters 11–21)
Romans
Four Men of God (Abraham, Joseph, Moses, David)
1 and 2 Peter (Letters to People in Trouble)
Genesis (Chapters 1–13)

Groups Reaching People from Non-Christian Cultures

Genesis (Chapters 1–13)
Mark
Romans
Four Men of God (Abraham, Joseph, Moses, David)
Philippians and Colossians (Letters from Prison)
Patterns for Living with God (Twelve Old Testament Character Studies)

Church Groups

Genesis (Chapters 1–13)
Matthew, Book 1 (Chapters 1–16)
Matthew, Book 2 (Chapters 17–28)
1 Corinthians (Challenge to Maturity)
2 Corinthians and Galatians (A Call for Help and Freedom)
1 and 2 Peter (Letters to People in Trouble)
Psalms and Proverbs
Four Men of God (Abraham, Joseph, Moses, David)
Celebrate

Mission Concerns Groups
Luke
Acts
Ephesians and Philemon
The Coming of the Lord (1 and 2
   Thessalonians, 2 and 3 John, Jude)
Romans
1 John and James
Amos (Prophet of Life-Style)

Advanced Groups
Courage to Cope
They Met Jesus (Eight Studies of New
   Testament Characters)
Hebrews
Choose Life (Ten Studies of Basic
   Christian Doctrine)
Amos (Prophet of Life-Style)
The Coming of the Lord (1 and 2
   Thessalonians, 2 and 3 John, Jude)
Prophets of Hope (Haggai, Zechariah,
   Malachi)

Adult and older teens
Matthew, Book 1 (Chapters 1–16)
Matthew, Book 2 (Chapters 17–28)
They Met Jesus (Eight Studies of New
   Testament Characters)
Choose Life (Ten Studies of Basic
   Christian Doctrines)
Celebrate
Courage to Cope
Set Free
Patterns for Living with God (Twelve
   Old Testament Character Studies)

Biweekly or Monthly Groups
They Met Jesus (Eight Studies of New
   Testament Characters)
Set Free
Celebrate
Courage to Cope
Psalms and Proverbs

How to Start a Neighborhood Bible Study
(A Guide to Discussion Study) is also
   available.